A GUIDE TO THE CATHEDRAL CHURCI ST ANNE, BELFAST

St Anne's Cathedral – a Cathedral of the United Dioceses of Down and Dromore and the Diocese of Connor.

ISBN: 978-0-9573019-0-0

Text by Mr Norman Weatherall, photographs by Dr Paul Larmour, introduction and illustration captions by the Dean, the Very Revd John Mann.

This publication is a joint project of St Anne's Cathedral and the Good Bookshop.

Designed by Tonic Design, Belfast

A GUIDE TO THE CATHEDRAL CHURCH OF ST ANNE, BELFAST

O GRAVE WHERE IS THY VICTORY

CONTENTS

INTRODUCTION

St Anne's Cathedral has stood for over 100 years as a place of Christian worship in the heart of the City of Belfast. This guidebook will give you just a taste of what this wonderful building has to offer the visitor, the pilgrim and the regular attendee at daily and Sunday services.

Probably the most important visual art in the Cathedral are the mosaics (seven years work by two sisters Gertrude and Margaret Martin), the carved stonework (sculpted by Rosamond Praeger, Morris Harding and Esmond Burton), the many fine stained glass windows, the carefully sourced marble tiles on floor and walls and the delicate wood carving. Not to mention the lovely needlework in both cushions and kneelers, most of which was done by members of the Cathedral community.

The building itself is *Romanesque*, giving it a lofty grandeur associated with that style: semi-circular arches and massive pillars, vast and high single windows, and the whole possessing an uncluttered spacious-ness that draws us into awe and wonder at the greatness of God.

It is a living place where day by day the cycle of worship is maintained and which welcomes visitors as tourists, pilgrims, regular worshippers, or merely those who seek a quiet place to ponder alone.

I am grateful to all who have contributed to this guidebook, to the Friends of the Cathedral and the Good Bookshop that have funded its production, to Dr Paul Larmour for his photographs and to Mr Norman Weatherall for the text.

Thank you for buying this guidebook. I hope it will remind you of a happy visit to our Cathedral and City.

John Mann (Dean)

A GREAT ADVANTAGE TO BELFAST

Statement regarding a proposed Cathedral for Belfast (1896)

"The want of a stately and commodious Central Church for the United Diocese of Down and Connor and Dromore, and for the great and growing city of Belfast, has been long and generally admitted.

The advantages which such a Church would confer on the members of the Church of Ireland in Ulster, and upon the cause of religion generally in the Northern Province are obvious.

Belfast's status as 'a city' almost demands the acquisition of a cathedral, which is generally associated as a necessary qualification with towns which are so dignified.

There is no Church in the city in a central position capable of accommodating large congregations for important services or festivals, and structurally suitable for ordinations, visitations, and other functions of a Metropolitan or Diocesan Church.

From a religious point of view, the influence of such a building, and its services, cannot but be very great.

Its gates shall not be shut at all by day, and it shall be open and free to every weary sinner who would seek his Saviour's presence, or supplicate his heavenly Father's blessing.

From an aesthetic point of view, the acquisition of such a building...will be a great advantage to Belfast; while its erection on the site proposed...cannot fail to exert a wholesome moral influence on a district whose present condition is by no means satisfactory."

OLD ST ANNE'S CHURCH

The site of the new proposed Cathedral

People

Built 1774-1776, the church was a gift to Belfast by the landlord, *Lord Donegall,* who chose to call it St Anne's in honour of his wife, *Lady Anne,* nee Hamilton. Anne is the name traditionally given to the mother of the Virgin Mary, who is the patron saint of Canada and Brittany.

Architect *Francis Horne* of Warwick and local builder *Roger Mulholland* oversaw the erection of the church.

The 1819 Belfast directory noted: "Through the ignorance of an English architect, in connecting the framework of the foundations of the tower with that of the body of the house, the former, by its greater weight, sunk deeper, and occasioned rents in the superstructure which rendered it unsafe to finish the upper part of the tower with stone. It was, therefore, carried up with timber, and the intention of the late *Marquis of Donegall* to introduce a set of bells was frustrated."

Architecture

Structural problems made it necessary to take down the church's West Front in the 1830s and was rebuilt in a different design.

The church was demolished early in 1904 to make way for the new cathedral which was already rising around the old building. In answer to those who regretted its passing, the cathedral architect, *Thomas Drew,* said: "Its cramped galleried interior is not of noble design. Its four square walls of rough brick and its wooden window sashes have served out their time. Its only feature of architectural merit is a Tower Cupola which is for the most part of wood. Its match-boarding and framing have been only maintained with much renewal of carpentry and painting ... The frontispiece portico is not of much architectural merit, and it, too, is of much decayed Scrabo stone that has lasted its time. The whole building has sunk, like most buildings in the yielding soil of Belfast, until its floor is on the level of the ground and the steps on which it may have been elevated have long disappeared."

THE NAVE

Opened for Public Worship in 1904

The cathedral was intended to be a place in which large congregations would meet on great Church occasions. Therefore, the Nave (from the Latin, *Navis*, meaning 'a ship'), stretched from the West Front to the steps of the choir, was the first part to be opened for public worship, on 2nd June 1904.

Architecture

The foundation stone of the cathedral was laid in September 1899 and building work began round the old church which remained in use until it was demolished at the end of 1903.

Thomas Drew and *W.H.Lynn*, both Belfastmen, had been appointed architects, Drew taking the leading role. The style chosen for the cathedral was *Romanesque*, characterised by semi-circular arches to doors and windows.

Further sections would be erected as money became available. It took nearly 80 years for the project to be completed: Crypt and foundations for a proposed Crossing Tower 1922-24; Apse and Ambulatory 1959; South Transept 1974; North Transept 1981. A temporary brick Chancel did duty until the East End was completed. The stainless steel Spire was lowered into place in 2007.

The nature of the site meant that wooden piles, four double rows, up to fifty feet long, had to be driven through the underlying bed of soft clay (Sleech) to provide a foundation for the walls and pillars.

At first the Nave was very plain: a concrete floor, a few stained glass windows, no sculptures. Floor, windows and carvings were added as individuals and organisations offered them as memorials.

In the central area of the floor at the West End is a black and white marble maze, or labyrinth, representing the journey of life. Following the white route (virtue) leads the pilgrim into the main Aisle proceeding to the Altar. However the black route leads nowhere.

The massive pillars of the Nave have very elaborately carved capitals. These are all different and bear close inspection. Industries connected to Belfast, from shipbuilding to linen production are depicted with other features built around individuals, organisations or themes, such as 'music' or 'motherhood'. The basilica style of the Cathedral, so unusual in Ireland, is reflected in these five pillars on each side, and with half pillars built into the west wall, with the four archangels carved in the four corners of the central part of the Nave: Gabriel, Michael, Raphael and Uriel.

Above: The nave looking from the south-west corner, showing the hassocks or kneelers all different and hand sewn. The arches are of the characteristic semi-circular pattern of the overall Romanesque design of the building.

These Volumes in which are recorded the names of Irishmen who
fell in the Great War were given to Belfast Cathedral by
the Irish National War Memorial Committee.

SAMUEL

NORTH AISLE

Leading to the Regimental Chapel and Ambulatory

Stained Glass Windows

The rose coloured window in the West Front depicts Moses raising a bronze serpent in the wilderness so that whoever had been bitten by a snake may look at the staff and be healed (NUMBERS 21). This window and the carving of the crucifixion outside, above the *North Door*, are related as type and antitype in an interpretation of scripture whereby an Old Testament event is seen to foreshadow an event in the New Testament. *(also see p.39)*

The windows depict five major figures from the Old Testament: Samuel, Daniel, Nehemiah, Gideon and Jonathan. Each window has three parts: middle, the Old Testament figure; base, an event in the figure's story; top, an appropriate symbol.

The windows to the right and left tell the story of the building of the Temple in Jerusalem. On the left is King David whose wish to build a temple was denied (2 SAMUEL 7); on the right is Solomon, David's son and successor, who built the first temple (1 KINGS 6). In the middle window is Jesus Christ, the Living Temple of the New Jerusalem, (REVELATION 21).

Remembering the Great War

On the left of the aisle the War Memorial Lectern whose eight volumes contain the names of some forty-nine thousand, five hundred Irish soldiers killed in the Great War 1914-1918. Above the great west doors is a mosaic (musical angels) commemorating choirmen who lost their lives in the Great War.

Below: A characteristically complex detail of one of the nave windows. All are based on Old Testament figures. Here Samuel as an old man is teaching the young.

Opposite: Jonathan, son of Saul, loved by David whom he saved from the wrath and jealousy of his father. Jonathan perished in battle at the side of Saul.

JONATHAN
THERE IS NO RESTRAINT TO THE LORD TO SAVE BY MANY OR BY FEW
TO THE GLORY OF GOD AND IN MEMORY OF THE MEMBERS
OF THE QUEENS ISLAND UNIONIST CLUB WHO GAVE
THEIR LIVES FOR THEIR COUNTRY IN THE GREAT WAR

Age
At the
remember
them

THE REGIMENTAL CHAPEL

The Chapel of the Royal Irish Regiment

The Chapel is the spiritual home of the Royal Irish Regiment. To be found there are memorial books, chairs and kneelers donated by families in memory of fallen comrades, a list of men honoured with the Victoria Cross and regimental flags.

The Font is a memorial to a number of soldiers killed on active service in the Palestine Conflict, 1937-1939.

In the glass case on the left, entering from the Nave, is the Majury Prayerbook, whose story is told in the accompanying newspaper report. A facsimile has been attached to the display case. *Major General Majury*, along with the late *Dean Sammy Crooks*, was a key figure in the establishment of the Chapel.

The Cathedral Organ

Across the Chancel, from the Chapel, there is a good view of the Cathedral Organ which has four manuals and seventy speaking stops. Originally built in 1907, the organ was reconstructed and relocated to its present position in 1975 and is the work of *Messrs Harrison and Harrison of Durham.*

VII/X
THE ROYAL IRISH RANGERS CHAPEL
DEDICATED ON 6TH JUNE 1981
BY
THE LORD BISHOP OF CONNOR
THE RIGHT REVEREND A. H. BUTLER
HON. CHAPLAIN THE ROYAL IRISH RANGERS
S. B. CROOKS, DEAN
MAJOR-GENERAL H. E. N. BREDIN
COLONEL OF THE REGIMENT
THE NORTH TRANSEPT
THE LORD BISHOP OF CONNOR
THE RIGHT REVEREND A. H. BUTLER

OWN BEAST AND BROUGHT HIM TO AN INN AND TOOK
WHEN HE SAW HIM PASSED BY ON THE OTHER SIDE LIKEWISE

AMBULATORY

Designed by John McGeagh, 1959

The Ambulatory, from the Latin *ambulare*, to walk, provides a link between the North and South Aisles. In a medieval cathedral the main shrine would have been located behind the High Altar and pilgrims could have approached it via either aisle without disturbing a service being conducted in the Nave.

Stained Glass Windows

Features of the ambulatory include the windows which illustrate five of St Paul's Fruits of the Spirit (Galatians 5): Peace (Royal Ulster Constabulary George Cross), Patience (Prison Officers Association), Charity (in memory of *Dean Sammy Crooks*), Faith and Joy. The triple window behind the altar depicts the story of the Good Samaritan and is the oldest in the building. It came from the old St Anne's Church to which it was given in memory of *Sir William Johnston*, Mayor of Belfast in 1849 when *Queen Victoria* paid her only visit to the town. Other windows commemorate military medical services.

Memorials

Kegworth Air Disaster, 8th January, 1989; Coventry Cross of Nails; books belonging to the bereavement counselling organisation Remember our Child. "The Breastplate of St Patrick" (in the small glass case) is the work of *Charles Braithwaite*, a Belfast artist and teacher.

Photographs show choir and clergy at various times, and one poignant image of the Cathedral standing proud while around it Donegall Street has been reduced to rubble in an air raid (1941).

Pictures

Portraits depict three nineteenth century bishops of Down and Connor and Dromore: *Richard Mant*, hymnwriter and historian; *Robert Knox*, later Archbishop of Armagh; William Reeves, antiquarian.

The Treasury

On display are vessels regularly used in cathedral services. Among them are items which came to St Anne's when the Corporation Church was closed in 1774. These include a paten, dated around 1650, and the 1743 Claudius Gilbert flagons. The bowl on display contained the soil which was scattered on *Lord Edward Carson*'s coffin. The soil was taken from the six counties of Northern Ireland and the cemetery at St Columb's Cathedral, Londonderry. It is now used occasionally at baptisms.

Opposite: Windows in the Ambulatory are themed on the great virtues, of which Patience is featured in that presented by the Northern Ireland Prison Service. The figure of Job is shown in the central orb.

Below: The beautiful Rosamond Praeger carving on the north side of the Ambulatory picks up the Christian interpretation of the Isaiah text, 'In the shadow of the great rock' as being under the protection of Christ

PATIENCE
To the Glory of GOD and in memory of colleagues
who served in the Northern Ireland Prison Service

CHARITY

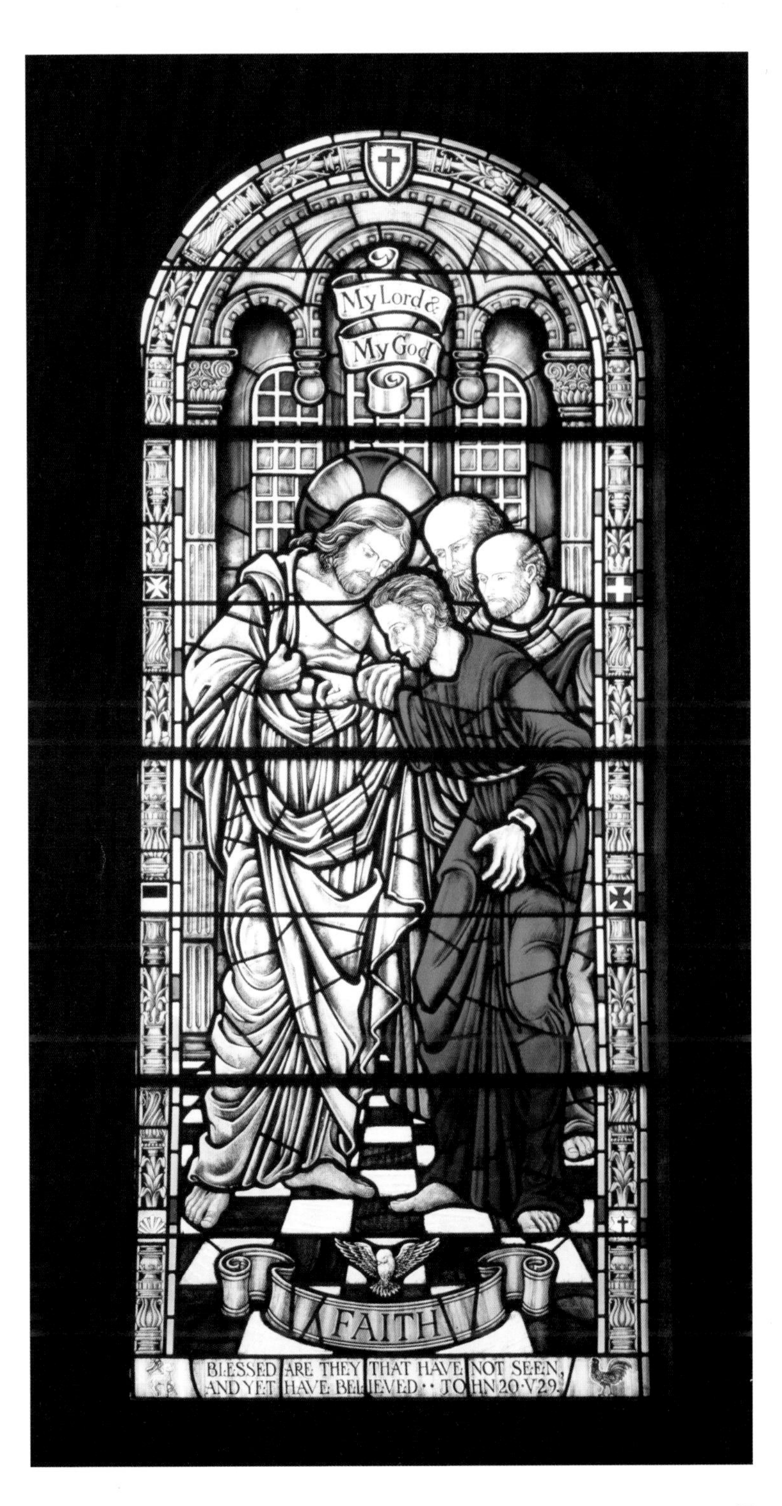
My Lord &
My God
FAITH
BLESSED ARE THEY THAT HAVE NOT SEEN,
AND YET HAVE BELIEVED · · JOHN 20·V 29.

SANCTUARY AND CHOIR

The Heart of the Cathedral

The Altar

The central act of the Christian faith, the Eucharist, or Holy Communion is celebrated at the Altar on which are carved the Instruments of the Passion of Christ – nails, a crown of thorns, whips, a rod with a sponge of drugged wine, and the spear thrust into Our Lord's side. In the centre is the sacred monogram, a shortened form of *Jesus* in Greek, *IHS*. The frontal features are depicted in the seasonal colours of the Church's year: violet (Advent and Lent), gold (Christmas, Epiphany and Easter) green (Trinity), red (Pentecost, martyrs).

The Chancel

To the left and right is a bishop's throne or *cathedra*, a word of Greek origin, from which derives the word cathedral. When the cathedral was founded Connor, Down and Dromore constituted a single diocese. In 1944 Connor was separated from Down and Dromore, hence the two episcopal seats. The chapter canons are drawn from both dioceses and their stalls form the back row of the Chancel on each side.

The Clerestory windows, the only abstract art in the cathedral, were the work of *Edward Marr*, late of Belfast College of Art and the gift of *Sir Robert Ernest Herdman* in memory of his wife, *Lucy Herdman* in 1976. From left to right they represent creation, the Trinity and the Eucharist.

The Spire

The Nave was consecrated in 1904, and to celebrate the centenary of this event a competition was organised to design a Spire for the cathedral. The chosen entry was submitted by *Colin Conn Architects*, Belfast. *The Spire of Hope*, manufactured in Switzerland from stainless steel, rises 250 feet (c.76m) above street level. The dedication took place on September 11th, 2007, when the preacher was the *Right Reverend Doctor Mark Sisk*, Bishop of New York.

Above: A striking window created in the Belfast College of Art by Edward Marr depicting the industry of the ity upon which is superimposed a chalice, symbolic of the life of Christ.

Opposite: The centre of the three abstract windows high above the Cathedral's altar. This image represents the Trinity: The Father as the light of the sun, the Holy Spirit as a dove in the centre, whilst a crown of thorns can be picked out at the bottom.

OIKOUMENE

THE CHAPEL OF UNITY

South Transept completed in 1974

Oikumene

Behind the Altar are symbols of the World Council of Churches. A ship, with the mast and spar forming a cross, the dove, representing peace and a Greek word, *oikumene* meaning the whole inhabited world. Oecumenism is illustrated on the kneelers: the interlacing designs signify unity, but no two are the same: the oecumenical movement aims at unity, but not uniformity. The kneelers here and throughout the building are the work of the Tapestry Guild. On the oecumenical front, Belfast Cathedral and St Peter's Roman Catholic Cathedral, formed The Cathedral Partnership in 1998.

Stained Glass Windows

The windows bear the emblems of the Church Lads' Brigade, Scout Association, Girl Guides and Girls' Brigade. *William McVicker,* who introduced the Boy's Brigade to Ireland in 1888, is remembered by a plaque.

Looking from the Chapel of Unity upwards and towards the north transept, the largest window of the Cathedral is to be seen high in the Military Chapel. The circular shadow behind the window is cast by the tallest celtic cross in Ireland, in the gable outside. Above the Chapel of Unity is the organ, whilst unseen, beneath the Chapel, in part of the crypt, there is the Chapel of the Faithful Departed, consecrated in 2011, where ashes may be placed following cremation.

SOUTH AISLE

A Celebration of Life after Death

The South Aisle holds the only tomb in the cathedral, that of *Edward Carson*, lawyer, parliamentarian and leader of Unionist opposition to Home Rule for Ireland from 1910 to 1921, buried here on 20th October 1935.

Stained Glass Windows

Approached from the East End the windows portray five more Old Testament figures: David, Abraham, Moses, Joseph and Joshua.

The rose coloured South Aisle window in the West Front illustrates a scene from the story of Jonah as he is 'resurrected' after three days in the belly of the whale. Outside, above the porch, there is a representation of the Resurrection of Jesus Christ.

The butterflies in the window are ancient symbols of resurrection (the chrysalis representing death and the butterfly new life), the brevity of human life and the soul.

Above: A carved capital by Morris Harding.

Below: A bronze plaque by Rosamund Praeger depicting Lord Carson, the only person buried in the Cathedral.

Opposite: One of the large South Aisle Nave windows depicting Moses.

THE BAPTISTRY

Observed from the 'Mother and Child' on the Pillar of Womanhood

Since baptism is the rite by which one enters and is made a member of the Church the practice was adopted of placing the Baptistry close to the entrance to the church building.

The structural part of the Baptistry was designed by *W.H.Lynn* and completed in 1924 under the supervision of *R.M.Close*. The interior decoration, floor, mosaic, capitals and Font, as designed by *Sir Charles Nicholson*.

The Font

This was presented by the children of the united diocese of Down and Connor and Dromore and subscribers who had been baptised in the old church. The meaning of baptism is given in the colours of the Font: the black stonework represents sin, the red columns repentance and the white (Portland and alabaster) grace.

The mosaic symbolises creation: the classical elements of water, earth, air and fire are depicted. God's hand blesses His creation. The geometric pattern on the floor is in a style known as *Opus Alexandrinum*.

Stained Glass Windows

The windows illustrate baptismal occasions. The figure of a white Friar is to be found in the bottom right hand corner of the window showing St Patrick baptising and is the trademark of the maker of the Baptistry and Nave windows, *James Powell*, of the Whitefriars Glassworks, London.

Above: A feature of one of the windows of the baptistry. The simplicity of the central angelic figure holding a pure white cloth beside the font should not distract us from the wealth and variety of detail surrounding it.

Opposite: More than 150,000 pieces of glass tesserae are said to make up this spectacular mosaic of creation on the ceiling of the baptistry. The work of the sisters Gertrude and Margaret Martin, who created all the mosaics in St Anne's over a period of seven years.

THE CHAPEL OF THE HOLY SPIRIT

The oldest and finest of the four Cathedral Chapels

In the north west corner of the nave, close to the north door and opposite the baptistry is the Chapel of the Holy Spirit which was added in the 1920's. It has windows depicting the presence of the Holy Spirit from God's act of Creation to the vision of St John in Revelation. The annunciation to the Blessed Virgin Mary and the baptism of Jesus by John in the River Jordan are shown in windows in the north wall, whilst the scene of the Upper Room on the Day of Pentecost is to be seen above the altar.

The glory of this small Chapel is accentuated by the gold mosaic ceiling; the angelic and spiritual presence suggesting the attention of the Holy Spirit to the life of all people and the whole of Creation is striking.

WEST FRONT

Dedicated to the memory of Ulster's War Heroes

The West Front is a modified version by *Sir Charles Nicholson* of *Thomas Drew*'s original design. Completed in 1927, the West Front is a memorial to those who fought in the the First World War (1914-1918) and as an offering of thanks for victory in that conflict. The bronze doors were also designed by *Charles Nicholson* and made by the Tudor Art Company, London in 1929.

Sculptures

The North Porch tympanum carries a sacrificial depiction of the Crucifixion of Our Lord,"He that loseth his life shall save it."; the South Porch, the Resurrection and victory over death, "O Grave where is thy Victory?"

This triumph of peace and righteousness is represented above the Central West Door by an enthroned Christ surrounded by saints, his right hand raised in blessing, his left holding the Book of Life, his foot treading upon the powers of darkness in the form of a winged serpent.

Below this arcade are four sculptures representing (from the left) toil, strife, love and avarice.

Above: The scene of Christ's victory over sin and death carved on the tympanum above the central great West Door to the Cathedral by Mr Esmond Burton.

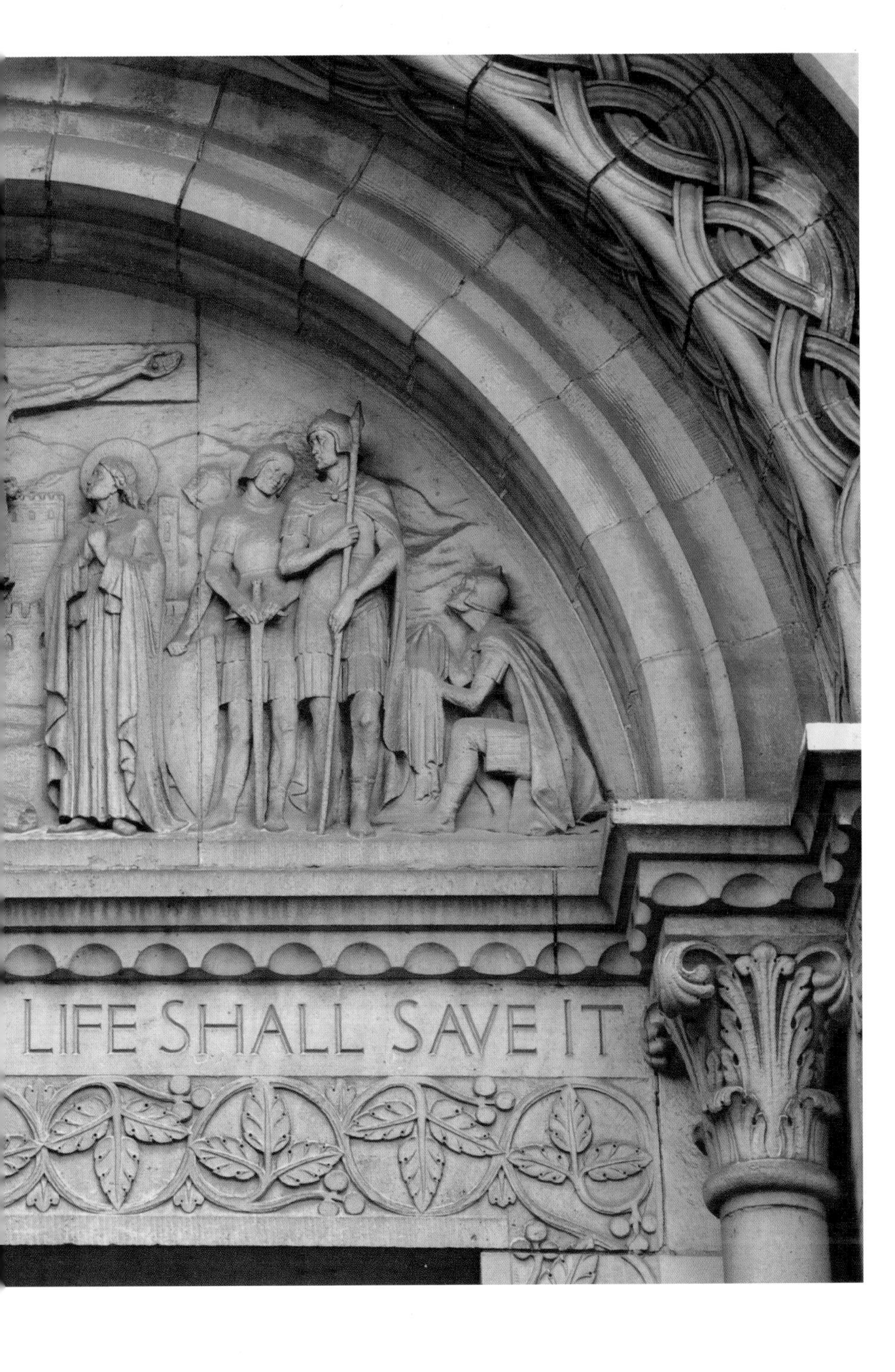
LIFE SHALL SAVE IT

TIMELINE

A historic timeline of St Anne's Cathedral

1774 Starting the construction of the Old St Anne's Church.

1776 Completion of the Old St Anne's Church construction.

1830s Rebuilding of the West Front.

1888 Introduction of the Boy's Brigade to Ireland.

1896 Statement Regarding a Proposed Cathedral for Belfast.

1899 Foundation stone of the Cathedral laid.

1904 The Old St Anne's Church demolished and construction of the new Cathedral begun.

Consecration of the Nave.

The new Cathedral Nave opened public worship for the first time.

1907 Building of the Cathedral Organ.

1912 The sinking of the Titanic (15th April)

1914 British declaration of war against Germany (August 4th)

1918 Armistice signed to end the fighting of the Great War.

1921 Formation of the Home Rule Parliament of Northern Ireland, heavily influenced by Edward Carson.

1924 Completion of the Crypt and foundations for a proposed crossing tower.

1927 Completion of the West Front.

1928 Dedication of the Baptistry?

1929 Instalment of the West Front bronze doors.

Wall Street Crash, plunging the world into depression. (October)

1932 The Chapel of the Holy Spirit built and consecrated to mark the 1500th anniversary of St Patrick coming to Ireland.

1935 Burial of Edward Carson in the South Aisle. (October 20th)

1937 Arab Revolt in Palestine.

1939 Declaration of War against Germany. (3rd September)

1944 Separation of the diocese of Connor from Down and Dromore into two diocese.

1945 VE Day (Victory in Europe) to celebrate the unconditional surrender of the German armed forces. (8th May)

1952 Princess Elizabeth becomes Queen aged 25. (February 7th)

1953 Coronation of Queen Elizabeth II.

1959 Apse and Ambulatory completed.

1974 South Transept completed.

1975 Relocation of the Cathedral organ to the current position.

1976 Presentation of the Clerestory windows.

1981 North Transept completed.

Consecration of The Regimental Chapel of the Royal Irish Rangers and the Royal Irish Regiment on the anniversary of D-Day. (June 2nd)

1998 The Cathedral Partnership formed between Belfast Cathedral and St Peter's Roman Catholic Cathedral

Good Friday Agreement between the British and Irish governments.

2001 Terrorist attack on the The World Trade Centre, New York. (September 11th)

2007 Dedication of the Spire of Hope.

NOTES & SKETCHES

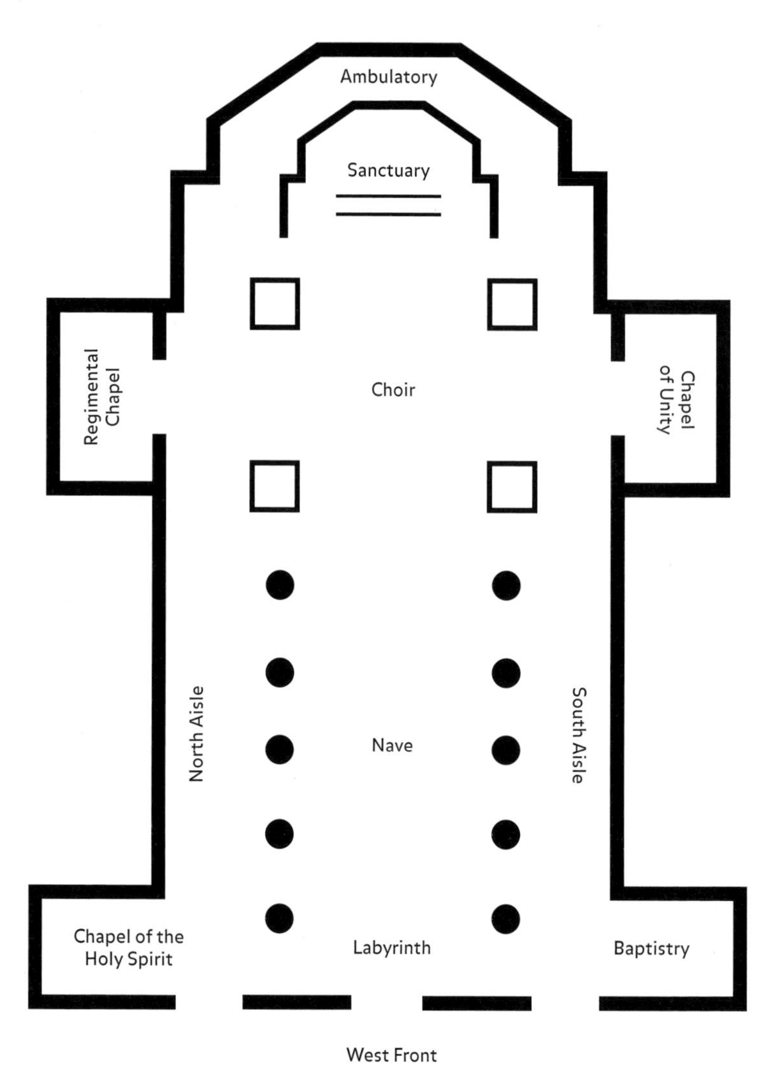
Ambulatory
Sanctuary
Regimental Chapel
Choir
Chapel of Unity
North Aisle
Nave
South Aisle
Chapel of the Holy Spirit
Labyrinth
Baptistry
West Front